I WONDER Why

Penguins Can't Fly

and other questions
about polar lands

Pat Jacobs

KINGFISHER
NEW YORK

KINGFISHER
LONDON & NEW YORK

Copyright © 2011 by Macmillan Publishers International Ltd
Published in the United States by Kingfisher,
175 Fifth Ave., New York, NY 10010
Kingfisher is an imprint of Macmillan Children's Books,
London.
All rights reserved.

Distributed in the U.S. and Canada by Macmillan,
175 Fifth Ave., New York, NY 10010

Library of Congress Cataloging-in-Publication data has been
applied for.

ISBN 978-0-7534-6518-9 (HC)
ISBN 978-0-7534-6530-1 (PB)

Kingfisher books are available for special promotions and
premiums. For details contact: Special Markets Department,
Macmillan, 175 Fifth Ave., New York, NY 10010.

For more information, please visit www.kingfisherbooks.com

Printed in China
11
11TR/0319/WKT/UNTD/128MA

Consultant: David Burnie
Illustrations: Martin Camm 6–7, 9bl, 14–15, 16–17, 18–19,
20–21, 22–23, 24–25, 26–27, 30–31; Phil Jacobs 4–5, 8–9,
10–11, 28bl, 29br, 30br, 31br; Peter Wilks (Plum Pudding)
all cartoons.

Cover: An arctic tern flies over a group of Emperor penguins
and a leaping gentoo penguin.

CONTENTS

Where are the poles?

The North Pole lies at the center of the Arctic Circle. At the North Pole, wherever you turn, you will be facing south. The South Pole is at the opposite end of Earth, in the middle of the Antarctic Circle on the continent of Antarctica.

Antarctic Circle

geographic South Pole

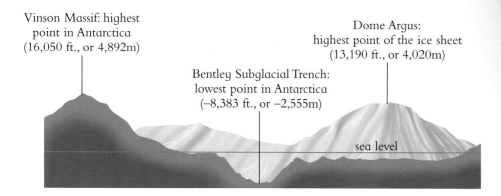

Vinson Massif: highest point in Antarctica (16,050 ft., or 4,892m)

Bentley Subglacial Trench: lowest point in Antarctica (−8,383 ft., or −2,555m)

Dome Argus: highest point of the ice sheet (13,190 ft., or 4,020m)

sea level

Why is Antarctica the highest and lowest continent?

The thick ice sheet makes Antarctica the world's highest continent, with an average height of 7,900 feet (2,400m). At 8,383 feet (2,555m) below sea level, the Bentley Subglacial Trench in west Antarctica is the lowest place on Earth that is not underwater.

At the poles, the sun rises and sets only once a year, so a day lasts for 12 months. Because Earth is tilted, one pole faces the Sun for six months while the other pole is dark, and then the opposite pole has six months of daylight.

Good night!

geographic North Pole

Arctic Circle

Why are there four poles?

Earth is a giant magnet, which is why a compass points to the North Pole. The geographic North and South poles are fixed points, but because Earth's magnetic field is always changing, the magnetic North and South poles move every day.

magnetic North Pole

How could north become south?

North Pole

Every so often, Earth's magnetic field reverses, so a compass that pointed north would then point south. This last occurred more than 780,000 years ago, and scientists think that it is due to happen again.

Can deserts be snowy?

Very cold air cannot hold much water, so it rarely snows at the poles. Parts of the Arctic are as dry as the Sahara Desert, and Antarctica is the driest continent on Earth. In fact, it the world's biggest desert.

a camel in the Sahara—the world's largest hot desert

Were the poles always frozen?

About 100–65 million years ago, the climate was warmer than it is today and the polar icecaps did not exist. Forests reached as far as the South Pole and were home to dinosaurs such as Antarctopelta (left).

Antarctica is the world's windiest place. The winds that blow around the coast can reach speeds of about 190 miles per hour (300km/h).

How cold are the poles?

In Antarctica in 1983, a temperature of −128.6°F (−89.2°C) was recorded—cold enough to freeze the mercury in a thermometer. The winter temperature at the North Pole averages −29°F (−34°C). That is 30°F (17°C) colder than a freezer.

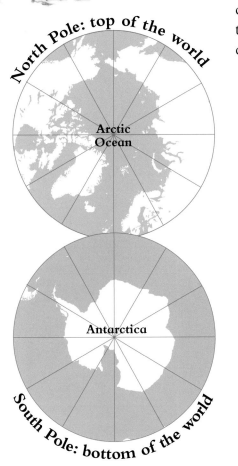

a polar bear in the Arctic— the world's second-largest cold desert

North Pole: top of the world

Arctic Ocean

Antarctica

South Pole: bottom of the world

Why is Antarctica colder than the Arctic?

Antarctica is a continent surrounded by the sea, while the Arctic is an ocean surrounded by land. Water stays warmer than land during the winter, so, on average, Antarctica is about 30°F (17°C) colder than the Arctic.

How are icebergs formed?

Icebergs are huge blocks of freshwater ice that break off from glaciers or from the ice shelf and float out to sea. The largest known iceberg was bigger than the island of Jamaica, and the tallest was the height of a 55-story building.

How thick is polar ice?

Sea ice in the Arctic is about 10 feet (3m) thick during the winter. The thickest ice is found in the Bentley Subglacial Trench, the lowest point in Antarctica. There the ice measures up to 15,670 feet (4,776m)—that is almost six times the height of the Burj Khalifa in Dubai.

At 2,717 feet (828m), the Burj Khalifa, in Dubai, United Arab Emirates, is the tallest building in the world.

Ice flows slowly from the center of Antarctica to the coast. An iceberg floating in the sea today could contain snow that fell on the South Pole during the time of the Neanderthals, early humans who lived about 100,000 years ago.

Only about one-eighth of an iceberg can be seen. The rest is hidden below the water.

Small icebergs are called growlers because they often make a growling noise as trapped air escapes from the ice.

What is permafrost?

Permafrost is ground that is frozen all year long. In 2007, a perfectly preserved baby mammoth, thought to have died 10,000 years ago, was unearthed from the permafrost in Siberia, Russia.

What lights up the sky?

The solar wind carries electrically charged particles from the Sun toward Earth. Some particles enter our atmosphere above the magnetic poles and collide with Earth's gases, creating a fantastic light show called the northern or southern lights.

What is diamond dust?

When the air temperature is very low, water vapor in the atmosphere freezes to form tiny ice crystals. These catch the Sun's light and sparkle like a sprinkling of diamonds in the sky.

A whiteout occurs when low white clouds cover the sky and the snow and sky merge into one. People say that it is like being trapped inside a huge white ball.

Which dogs are found at the poles?

A Brocken specter is a large ghostly figure with a rainbow halo. It is actually a person's shadow cast by a low Sun onto distant fog.

Sundogs are bright flares that appear on either side of the Sun when ice crystals in the sky reflect the sunlight. Moon dogs are sometimes seen, too, when the Moon is very bright.

Does anyone live in Antarctica?

No one lives there permanently, but Antarctica is visited by about 4,000 scientists during the summer. Only about 1,000 stay to brave the cold, dark winter, though.

Who first came to the poles?

American explorers Frederick Cook and Robert Peary both claimed to have reached the North Pole first—Cook in 1908 and Peary in 1909. Roald Amundsen led the first expedition to the South Pole, arriving in December 1911.

Early polar explorers used huskies to pull their sleds, but today dogs are banned from Antarctica to protect the wildlife.

Researchers at Antarctica's Concordia Research Station, studying the effects of living in space, are trying to find out if wearing socks at night would help astronauts sleep.

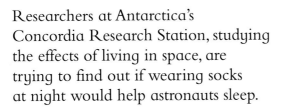

Do people still build igloos?

The word *iglu* means "house" in the Inuit language. So people in the Arctic do live in *iglus*, but igloos made of snow are now built only as temporary shelters during hunting trips.

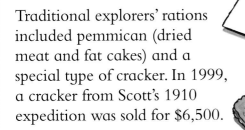

broken cracker
$6,500

Traditional explorers' rations included pemmican (dried meat and fat cakes) and a special type of cracker. In 1999, a cracker from Scott's 1910 expedition was sold for $6,500.

Norwegian Roald Amundsen reached the South Pole one month before Great Britain's Captain Robert Falcon Scott.

Are there any polar plants?

The poles are covered in ice all year long, but plants grow in less-cold areas called the tundra. For a few weeks in the middle of the summer, the Arctic tundra is carpeted in color as plants that have spent the winter beneath the snow burst into bloom.

The tundra's flowers attract many insects, so birds flock there during the summer to raise their families and make the most of the insect feast.

How do plants survive the cold?

Tundra plants huddle close to the ground in tight clumps and often have hairy leaves and stems to protect them from the cold. Cup-shaped flowers follow the Sun as it moves across the sky.

A snowy owl catches a lemming for its chicks.

Which tree grows in the "treeless" tundra?

The word *tundra* comes from a Finnish word meaning "treeless plain," so you would not expect to find any trees there. Yet a type of willow only 8 inches (20cm) tall has adapted to the cold, windy climate and provides food for caribou, muskoxen, Arctic hares, and lemmings.

Most owls are active only when it is dark, but snowy owls hunt in daylight, too—otherwise they would starve during the Arctic summer, when the Sun never sets.

Permafrost stops melting snow from sinking into the ground, so it forms pools of water that are perfect nurseries for mosquito larvae (young). Sometimes, the mosquito swarms are so large that they turn the sky gray.

In the summer, animals such as snowy owls and caribou take advantage of the plentiful food to raise their young and fatten up for the winter.

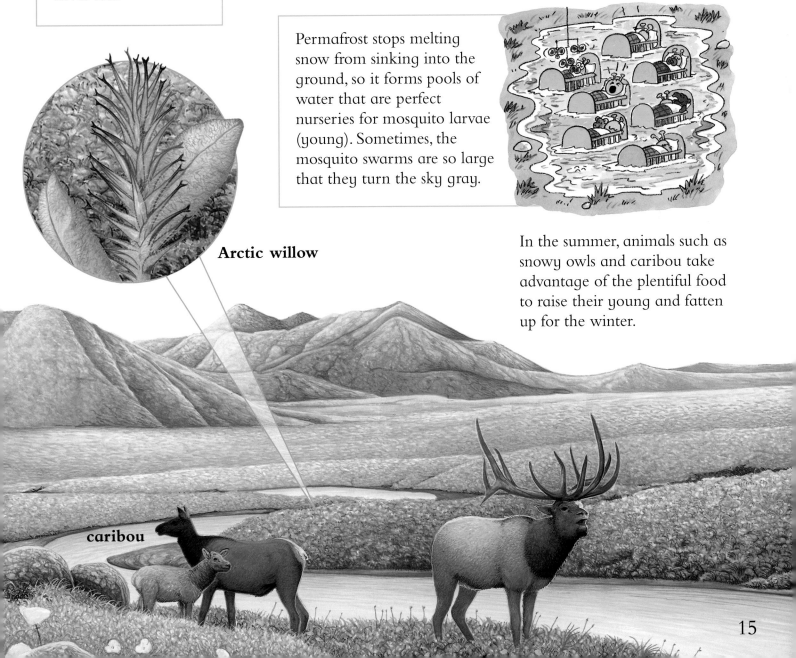

Arctic willow

caribou

How do animals survive the Arctic winter?

In the winter, temperatures in the Arctic drop to −58°F (−50°C), so polar animals grow a thick winter coat to keep them warm. The Arctic fox even has fur on the bottom of its feet and uses its bushy tail as a blanket.

Beneath its thick coat, the polar bear has black skin that absorbs heat from the Sun and keeps the animal warm.

An Arctic fox hears small animals moving in their underground burrows. It pounces to break through the snow and then grabs its prey.

Why aren't polar bears white?

If you plucked a few hairs from a polar bear, you would find that they are colorless. Like snow and ice, the hairs are translucent. Light passes through them, but they look white to us.

Collared lemmings are a favorite food for Arctic predators. A large family of Arctic foxes can eat up to 4,000 lemmings before the young leave the den.

Which creatures change color?

Arctic wolves, foxes, and ermines turn white in the winter so they can creep up on their prey without being seen. Arctic hares and collared lemmings grow white fur, too, so predators find them difficult to spot in the snow.

The Arctic ground squirrel hibernates from September to April to escape the winter cold. Its body temperature drops to 27°F (–3°C) during its seven-month sleep.

Which animal bullies bigger creatures?

The wolverine (below) is a fast and fierce hunter, armed with strong jaws and sharp claws. Arctic hares, squirrels, and birds are easy prey, but this dog-size predator also steals kills from bears and cougars and sometimes attacks much larger animals, such as caribou.

A wolverine steals food from a grizzly bear.

In the late summer, caribou stamp their feet, shake their heads, and run around wildly. They are trying to escape the warble flies that lay their eggs in the caribou's fur.

Although the Antarctic coastline is home to many birds and sea mammals, the largest creature that spends its whole life on land is a wingless fly, only 0.3 inches (7mm) long.

Actual size

How do muskoxen protect their young?

Adult muskoxen have sharp horns that can kill or injure the Arctic wolves that prey on the herd. When predators are nearby, the adults form a circle around the young, creating a spiky barricade with their horns.

Muskoxen have hardly changed since prehistoric times, when they lived alongside woolly mammoths and saber-toothed tigers.

Who puts puffins in danger?

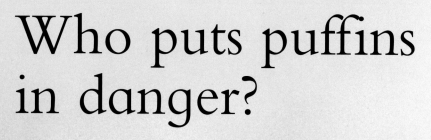

Puffins' natural predators include gulls, skuas, foxes, sharks, and killer whales, but humans are the greatest threat to their survival. Puffins feed on fish and other sea creatures, so they are endangered by overfishing and oil spills. In some places, people still eat puffins and their eggs.

Puffins have backward-pointing spines on their tongues and the tops of their mouths to hold onto their fishy catches. One puffin was seen with more than 60 fish in its beak.

A skua chases a kelp gull.

The wandering albatross is a superb flier with the widest wingspan of any bird, but it is very clumsy on land. It often turns somersaults as it crash-lands and regularly trips over its own feet.

Which bird migrates from pole to pole?

The Arctic tern breeds on the tundra and then flies to Antarctica as winter approaches. It makes the longest migration of any bird, traveling more than 21,750 miles (35,000km) each year.

Arctic tern

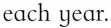

A skua attacks a penguin colony.

Although they have webbed feet, it seems that Arctic terns do not like the water. They swoop down to catch fish but do their best to avoid getting wet.

Are there pirates at the poles?

Skuas are nicknamed "pirates" because they steal food from other birds in midair. They target penguin colonies, too, often working in pairs. While one skua distracts a penguin, the other steals its egg or chick.

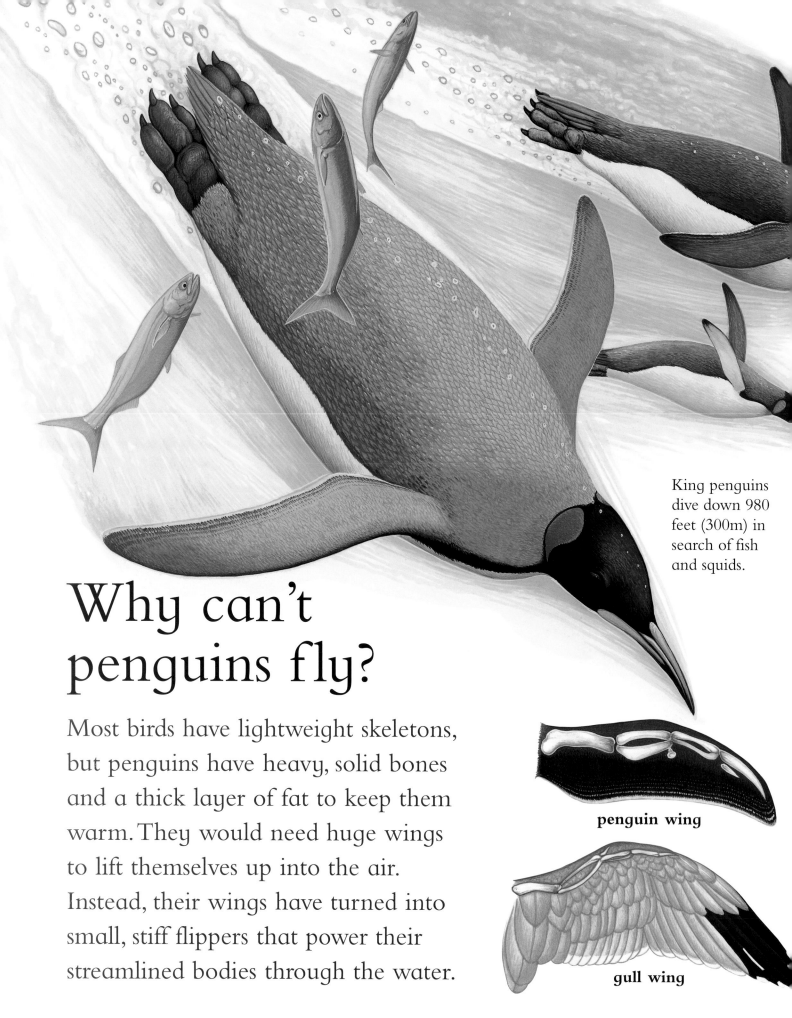

King penguins dive down 980 feet (300m) in search of fish and squids.

Why can't penguins fly?

Most birds have lightweight skeletons, but penguins have heavy, solid bones and a thick layer of fat to keep them warm. They would need huge wings to lift themselves up into the air. Instead, their wings have turned into small, stiff flippers that power their streamlined bodies through the water.

penguin wing

gull wing

Why don't polar bears eat penguins?

A polar bear would have to swim a long way to eat a penguin because they live at opposite ends of Earth. Polar bears live in the Arctic and penguins are found only south of the equator.

At five and a half feet (1.7m) tall, a penguin that waddled the earth around 40 million years ago could easily have pecked a man in the eye. Fossils of this Antarctic giant were found on Seymour Island.

Why don't penguins' eggs freeze?

An emperor penguin's egg would freeze in minutes if it were left on the ice, so the penguins balance their eggs on their feet and keep them warm inside a brood pouch. This is a flap of featherless skin that wraps around the egg.

Which seal is a champion diver?

Weddell seals dive down to 2,300 feet (700m) in search of fish and squids, and they can stay underwater for more than an hour. Their strong teeth help chew breathing holes in the ice, and they sometimes blow air into cracks in the ice to startle fish—which then swim right into the seals' mouths.

southernmost
seal

Weddell seals live in Antarctica, farther south than any other seal.

Polar fish have antifreeze in their blood to stop them from freezing solid. This fish antifreeze is sometimes used to stop ice crystals from forming in ice cream.

Where would you find a "bloodless" fish?

The crocodile icefish that lives in the sea around Antarctica has no red blood cells, so its blood is clear, just like water. The fish gets its name from its long snout, which is packed with white teeth.

Who is called the unicorn of the sea?

The male narwhal's unicorn-like tusk is actually an overgrown tooth. When the whale is one year old, one of his two top teeth grows through his lip. A ten-year-old narwhal's tusk can be 10 feet (3m) in length.

As walrus warm up in the sun, blood flows to the surface of their skin and they turn from muddy brown to pink.

25

Which hungry gulper eats four tons a day?

The blue whale is the biggest creature ever to have lived, yet it feeds on some of the smallest animals. Blue whales eat krill, swallowing more than four million each day during the summer months when they come to feed in polar waters.

Why are polar seas so lively?

The oceans around the poles are teeming with life. Cold water absorbs more oxygen, and currents carry nutrients to the surface, where they feed the phytoplankton—microscopic plants eaten by krill, which are an important food for many sea creatures.

sea squirt

Blue whales are not only big, they are very noisy, too. Their calls are louder than a jet engine and can be heard more than 500 miles (800km) away.

What are krill?

Krill are tiny, shrimplike animals that gather in swarms up to 4 miles (6km) long during the polar summers, often turning the water pink. One gallon (4L) of water can contain 250 krill.

The Antarctic seabed is home to many strange creatures, including sea squirts that look like glass tulips, huge starfish, and sea spiders the size of dinner plates, with up to 12 legs.

What does Antarctica tell us about space?

The only place colder than Antarctica is outer space, so it is the best place on Earth to test the space robots of the future. Underwater vehicle *Endurance* has been studying Lake Bonney, but one day it might explore the ocean that scientists believe lies beneath the icy crust of Europa, one of Jupiter's largest moons.

Why is Antarctica a meteorite hot spot?

There is nowhere better to search for meteorites, because they are so easy to see on the Antarctic ice sheet. *Nomad* is a robotic meteorite hunter that can tell the difference between a meteorite and a normal rock. Some of the meteorites it has found came from Mars.

Scientists have found large amounts of cosmic dust in Antarctic ice cores. They think the dust fell to Earth when a giant space rock exploded above the continent about 480,000 years ago.

Why is ice like a time machine?

Each layer of snow contains clues to what is happening in the world. By drilling out cores from polar ice, scientists can unlock the past and learn about volcanic eruptions, forest fires, dust storms, and temperature changes that occurred up to 750,000 years ago.

Because Antarctica is dark both day and night during the winter and the dry air is crystal clear, it is the best place in the world to view the stars.

Ice cores are long cylinders of compacted snow. They contain ash, dust, chemicals, radioactive substances, and even material from outer space.

Who pollutes the poles?

Sadly, human activities sometimes produce chemicals and oil spills that pollute our world. Winds and ocean currents may carry these pollutants to the poles, where they can harm the creatures that live there.

3. When polar bears eat the seals, poisons build up in their bodies.

1. Plankton absorb pollutants and are eaten by fish.

What is the ozone hole?

Ozone is a gas in our upper atmosphere that protects us from harmful ultraviolet rays from the Sun. Human-made chemicals can destroy ozone, and every spring the ozone layer above Antarctica has been getting thinner. A smaller ozone hole has recently appeared over the Arctic, too.

Antarctica

ozone hole in 2009

high ozone   low ozone

What if all of the polar ice melted?

If the polar icecaps melted, the sea would rise by about 200 feet (60m) and many low-lying countries would be flooded— but it would take thousands of years for this to happen.

2. Seals eat the fish and the harmful chemicals are stored in their fat.

Who lives where?

These lists are a guide to the natural habitat(s) of the animals shown in this book.

Arctic
Arctic fox
Arctic ground squirrel
Arctic hare
Arctic wolf
caribou (also called reindeer)
collared lemming
ermine
grizzly bear
muskox
narwhal
polar bear
puffin
snowy owl
walrus
wolverine

Antarctica
crocodile icefish
kelp gull
penguin
wandering albatross
Weddell seal

Arctic and Antarctica
Arctic tern
blue whale
krill
skua

31

Index